MW01595078

A Robbie Reader

Henry Ford

CARS FOR EVERYONE

by
Daryl Davis Zarzycki

Mitchell Lane
PUBLISHERS

P.O. Box 196
Hockessin, Delaware 19707
Visit us on the web: www.mitchelllane.com
Comments? email us: mitchelllane@mitchelllane.com

Printing 1   2   3   4   5   6   7   8   9

A Robbie Reader

Hillary Duff	Thomas Edison	Albert Einstein
Philo T. Farnsworth	**Henry Ford**	Robert Goddard
Mia Hamm	Tony Hawk	LeBron James
Donovan McNabb	Dr. Seuss	Charles Schulz

Library of Congress Cataloging-in-Publication Data
Zarzycki, Daryl.
   Henry Ford / by Daryl Davis Zarzycki.
      p. cm. — (A Robbie reader)
   Includes bibliographical references and index.
   ISBN 1-58415-301-6 (library bound)
   1. Ford, Henry, 1863–1947—Juvenile literature. 2. Automobile industry and trade—United States—Biography—Juvenile literature. 3. Industrialists—United States—Biography—Juvenile literature. 4. Automobile engineers—United States—Biography—Juvenile literature. I. Title. II. Series.
TL140.F6Z37   2004
338.7'6292'092—dc22

2004018360

ABOUT THE AUTHOR: Daryl Davis Zarycki is currently a reading specialist at Jennie Smith Elementary School in Newark, Delaware. She is married and has three grown children. She graduated from the University of Delaware with degrees in Elementary and Special Education. Her favorite subjects are science and math. And, of course, she loves to write.

PHOTO CREDITS: Cover, pp. 7, 11—Henry Ford Museum, The Edison Institute; pp. 12, 20—Library of Congress; pp. 4, 8, 16, 18, 20, 22, 25, 27, 28, 29—Collections of Henry Ford Museum and Greenfield Village; p. 15—Corel Corporation; p. 21—The National Automotive History Collection, Detroit Public Library; p. 25—Pat McCarthy; p. 29—AP Photos.

ACKNOWLEDGMENTS: The following story has been thoroughly researched, and to the best of our knowledge, represents a true story. While every possible effort has been made to ensure accuracy, the publisher will not assume liability for damages caused by inaccuracies in the data, and makes no warranty on the accuracy of the information contained herein.

TABLE OF CONTENTS

This is the first car Henry Ford built in 1896.

THE CHANGING WORLD

Do you know how long it takes to build one car today? For most models, each car takes less than 24 hours to build. Sixty cars can be made every hour. That's one car every minute! Times sure have changed. The first car Henry Ford made in 1896 took him three years to build.

Back in the 1700s, people made everything by hand. Watchmakers only made watches. Tailors made clothes. Because it took so long to make things by hand, the cost of each item was high.

People would learn one skill or trade, usually by being an apprentice (ah-PREN-tis).

Apprentices learned from trained workers. Once an apprentice mastered a skill, he or she could open a new shop.

In the 1800s, this process started to change. First, Eli Whitney invented a machine that removed the seeds from freshly picked cotton. His machine was called the cotton gin. The cotton gin saved time. People no longer had to pick the seeds out of the cotton by hand.

Other machines that made work easier were being invented. Soon factories **(FAK-toh-reez)** full of these machines were being built. Items could be made in factories faster than people could make them by hand. Factory workers formed an assembly **(ah-SEM-blee)** line. Each worker put one piece together. Then he or she passed the item to the next person, who would do the next step. The product would be passed down the line until it was complete.

In the early 1900s, Henry Ford made history. He made the assembly line better by adding a conveyor (**kon-VAY-or**) belt. Workers no longer had to pass parts down the line. The parts moved automatically.

Henry was first a farmer. Next he worked for a great inventor named Thomas Edison. Then he opened his own car factory. In 2003, Henry Ford's company sold almost 7 million cars. This is Henry's story.

Here is one of the first moving assembly lines.

Henry's father William   Henry's mother Mary

Henry at age 2 1/2

THE FORD FAMILY

In 1847, Henry's grandfather, John Ford, moved his wife and seven children from Ireland to America. A potato disease in Ireland left the family with little food and no crops to sell. Their trip to America by ship was hard. People became sick. Henry's grandmother died. Finally John Ford and his children arrived. They moved to Michigan. John then bought land and became a farmer.

When John's son William married Mary, they started their own farm. On July 30, 1863, their first son, Henry, was born in their farmhouse. Henry was the first of six children.

When Henry was seven, he started school in a one-room schoolhouse. His best friend there was Edsel Ruddiman. His favorite subject was math, but he was not a very good speller. At night, after the chores were done, Henry and his family would play cards. In the winter, Henry also enjoyed skating on the frozen creek with his brothers and sisters.

Henry loved going to the city. Most things that farmers needed could only be bought there. Henry would go along on the weekly trips.

Henry hated farm work. As the oldest, he had many chores to do. He fed the chickens, picked the apples, and filled the wood box. He hated plowing. He also hated the horses. He thought there must be a better way to move carts and things around. But how?

Henry started thinking about machines. His mother encouraged him to learn about them. He became good at putting things together. In fact, his brothers and sisters would hide their toys from him. He would love to take them apart just to see how they worked. But Henry's father thought he was just wasting his time. How would this tinkering help him with farming?

When Henry was 12, his mother died. He missed her terribly. His mother believed in him. His mother believed in his interest in machines.

Here Henry is plowing with the horses.

This is Henry Ford at age 23.

HENRY'S NEW LIFE

Henry's new life with machines began slowly. One day he took a trip to the city. He saw a wagon moving down the road. It was powered by a steam engine. One man shoveled coal into the boiler. Another man steered. Henry thought that this machine was great. A horse was not needed to move this wagon. Henry dreamed that one day he would make a machine that would travel the roads.

In 1879, Henry turned 16. He did not go back to school. He wanted to work with machines. He started as an apprentice at The Michigan Car Company. He was paid $1.10 a day. But Henry made a big mistake. Other workers had worked on a problem all day. Henry came and solved that problem in a few minutes. The workers were mad, and Henry was fired.

Next Henry worked at the James Flower & Brothers Machine Shop. He loved this job because the shop made many different products and machines. This company made valves and fire hydrants. It also made parts for engines out of iron and brass.

During his next job, Henry fixed steam engines. He still helped on his father's farm, using the steam engine for farm work. The steam engine did jobs that horses or people used to do. Henry worked hard. He loved traveling around repairing and using the steam engine.

Henry's father still hoped that Henry would become a farmer. And that almost happened! Henry met and fell in love with Clara Jane Bryant. They were married in 1888. Henry's father gave them 80 acres of farmland. His father told him that he could have the land as long as he would work on it and make it a good farm. Henry agreed. He chopped down trees from his land and ran a sawmill. At the sawmill, the logs were cut into lumber and then sold. The lumber was used for building.

A steam engine

Clara is helping Henry in his shop.

THE QUADRICYCLE

Henry still had his dream. He read about a new engine that worked without shoveling coal into a boiler. He also read about men who were building "horseless carriages." These were the very first cars. They used the new engines. He told Clara about his dream of making a machine that would travel the roads. She helped him follow his dream.

Henry wanted to learn all there was to know about these new engines. To do this, he and Clara moved to the city. In 1891, Henry started working for a company owned by Thomas Edison.

Henry's son Edsel

His job was to run the generators that gave electricity to customers. He was good at solving their problems. Finally, in 1896, Henry met the great inventor Thomas Edison. They became very good friends. Henry continued to do experiments with engines. He built a gas engine. Next, he wanted to build a car. He knew cars were his future.

Henry and Clara's son, Edsel, was born on November 6, 1893. Henry named his son after his good childhood friend. Edsel was their only child.

Henry knew that some people were now making cars. He wanted to make one that was better than all the rest. Building the car took him three years. His friends helped build it. One helped to make the starter. Another gave him spare parts from other cars.

Finally, Henry was ready to test his car. He called it a quadricycle **(QUAH-drih-sye-kul)**. It didn't look pretty. It was small and had four bicycle wheels. It had a gas engine and a seat.

There was no brake. It couldn't go backward. Henry started the engine, then slowly drove it down the street.

Henry, Clara, and grandson Henry Ford II are with the quadricycle.

Henry's quadricycle

Thomas Edison is sitting with Henry Ford. They were good friends.

A painting of Henry Ford

THE FORD COMPANY

In 1899, Henry sold his first car for $200. He remembered his dream of wanting to make a machine that would travel the roads. But now he wanted to make more. It would be risky. He already had a good job and a wonderful wife and son. Henry decided to start the Detroit Automobile Company. It didn't do well. In 15 months, the company built only 12 trucks. It went out of business.

Next, Henry found a group of people who liked his ideas. They gave him money to pay for a new factory. Together they started the Henry Ford Automobile Company. Henry had one problem. He wanted to build cars that most people could afford to buy. The cars needed to be built faster and cheaper. His partners wanted cars built for just rich people. Henry decided to leave this company.

Finally, on July 16, 1903, the Ford Motor Company was formed. By 1904, the company was making 1,700 cars a year. Many people wanted Ford's cars. The company could not make the cars fast enough. Cars had many moving parts. The assembly line would have to move faster. In 1913, the company started using a conveyor belt to carry the car parts down the assembly line. The assembly line became smoother and faster.

Henry's greatest car, the Model T, was nicknamed the Tin Lizzie. It was made of the best materials. Model Ts could be put together quickly, so the price of each was low. The first ones cost $850. In 1913, about 200,000 cars were sold. But in the 1920s, not as many people were buying the Model T, even though

Ford Motor Company was formed in 1903.

Here is the Model T car nicknamed "Tin Lizzie."

the price had dropped to less than $300. People wanted other cars in other colors. Henry did not want to change. He kept selling the Model T. At last, in 1927, Ford brought out a new model. His company stopped selling the Model T. The new Model A became a favorite.

Henry's son, Edsel, became president of the Ford Motor Company in 1919. He continued this job until his death in 1943. In 1945, Henry's grandson, Henry II, helped run the company.

In his later years, Henry formed the Ford Foundation. This foundation gave money to schools, museums, and hospitals.

In 1947, Henry Ford became sick. On April 7, he died. He was 84 years old. By this time, Henry had become very well known. Thousands of friends, family, and workers came to his funeral. His dream improved life for all of us. He helped to change our world forever.

Today you can visit the Henry Ford Museum in Dearborn, Michigan. It is called Greenfield Village. Henry Ford collected the buildings to put in the village. The village tells the story of the America he knew. You can tour the houses, schools, stores, and buildings where Henry lived, played, and worked.

Here are Edsel and Henry working together.

Ford's Model A car was first sold in 1927.

Here is Ford's 10 millionth car (on left) and his quadricycle (on right).

Many people attended Henry Ford's funeral.

1863	Henry Ford is born on July 30 in Greenfield Township, Michigan.
1876	His mother dies. Henry sees his first riding steam engine.
1882	Henry returns to family farm after doing apprenticeship.
1888	Henry marries Clara Jane Bryant.
1890	Henry begins experiments with "horseless carriage."
1891	He starts working for Edison Illuminating Company.
1896	Henry completes his first car, the quadricycle.
1901	He founds Henry Ford Automobile Company.
1903	The Ford Motor Company is incorporated.
1908	Begin producing Model T.
1913	Henry begins the first moving automobile assembly line.
1927	Begin producing Model A.
1943	Son Edsel dies.
1947	Henry Ford dies on April 7.

Books

Ford, Carin T. *Henry Ford: The Car Man.* New Jersey: Enslow Publishers, 2002.

Gourley, Catherine. *Wheels of Time: A Biography of Henry Ford.* Brookfield, CT: Milbrook Press, 1997.

Joseph, Paul. *Henry Ford.* Edina, Minn.: Abdo & Daughters, 1997.

Kent, Zachary. *The Story of Henry Ford and the Automobile.* Chicago, Ill.: Children's Press, Inc., 1990.

On the Web

"The Life of Henry Ford," http://www.thehenryford.org/exhibits/hf/default.asp

Spectrum: "Henry Ford," http://www.incwell.com/Biographies/Ford.html